Lessons *for* Living

JOHN PAUL II

Other Loyola Press books
by John Paul II

Go in Peace:
A Gift of Enduring Love

Lessons *for* Living

JOHN PAUL II

~

Edited by Joseph Durepos

LOYOLAPRESS.

CHICAGO

LOYOLAPRESS.

3441 N. ASHLAND AVENUE
CHICAGO, ILLINOIS 60657
(800) 621-1008
WWW.LOYOLABOOKS.ORG

John Paul II: Lessons for Living was selected, arranged, and edited by Joseph Durepos largely from materials originally published in *Celebrate the Third Millennium, Celebrate 2000,* and *The Prayers of Pope John Paul II,* edited by Paul Thigpen and published by Servant Publications, Inc.

All selections have been taken from the official Vatican translation of papal documents. Some are from encyclicals and apostolic letters published in the United States by Pauline Books & Media. Some texts appeared originally in *L'Osservatore Romano* (English edition, Via del Pellegrino, 00120 Vatican City, Europe), which is the official Vatican newspaper, and were reprinted in *The Pope Speaks (TPS),* a bimonthly periodical published by Our Sunday Visitor (200 Noll Plaza, Huntington, IN 46750). Used by permission. All rights reserved.

Scripture quotations contained herein are from the New Revised Standard Version of the Bible: Catholic Edition, copyright © 1993 and 1989 by the Division of Christian Education of the National Council of the Churches of Christ in the U.S.A. Used by permission. All rights reserved.

Excerpts from the English translation of the Catechism of the Catholic Church for Use in the United States of America, copyright 1994, United States Catholic Conference, Inc., Libreria Editrice Vaticana. Used with permission.

Cover design by Kathy Greenholdt
Interior design by Cynthia Dunne

Library of Congress Cataloging-in-Publication Data

John Paul II, Pope, 1920–
   John Paul II : lessons for living / edited by Joseph Durepos.
      p. cm.
   ISBN 0-8294-2059-2
   1. Catholic Church—Doctrines. 2. Christian life. I. Title: Lessons for living. II. Durepos, Joseph, 1955– III. Title.
BX1751.3.J635 2004
248.4'82—dc22

                                                                    2003024862

Printed in the United States of America
04 05 06 07 08 09 10 M-V 10 9 8 7 6 5 4 3 2

Contents

Contents

Contents

Contents

Foreword

The magnitude of John Paul II's accomplishments, and the sheer volume of his writings, can obscure a crucial fact about him. Within this great man—world statesman, theologian, philosopher, church leader—beats the heart of a pastor. John Paul II knows something about how men and women can find God. He understands much about how the power of God can be released in our lives. His supreme desire is that we come to embrace a faith that transforms the way we live, the way we relate to other people, the way we work.

This little book compiles John Paul II's essential pastoral wisdom. These are his most succinct and heartfelt thoughts about how we can draw closer to God and live as faithful, forceful Christians in a world that presents many challenges. I have made these selections from the pope's extensive writings and arranged them according to broad themes. Read these words from one of the church's greatest pastors. Ponder them. Let them penetrate your heart. They will draw you closer to God, because God is in them.

Joseph Durepos

1
A Hidden Treasure, an Open Book

Lord, reveal to all of us the interior world of
the soul, the hidden treasure within us, the
luminous castle of God. Make the exterior
world preserve the imprint of the Creator,
and may it be an open book that speaks to us
of God.

2
Humanity's Destiny

Humanity's destiny is written in the heart and mind of God, who directs the course of history. The Father puts in our hands the task of beginning to build here on earth the Kingdom of heaven that the Son came to announce and which will find its fulfillment at the end of time.

3
Immersed in This World

We live in history, side by side with our peers, sharing their worries and hopes. We cannot escape into another dimension, ignoring the tragedies of our era, closing our eyes and our hearts to the anguish that pervades life. On the contrary, we are immersed in this world every day, ready to hasten to wherever there is a brother or sister in need of help, a tear to be dried, a request for help to be answered.

4
Providence

The world and the events of history cannot be understood without professing faith in the God who is at work in them. Faith sharpens the inner eye, opening the mind to discover the workings of providence in the flux of events.

5
Faith and Reason

Faith and reason are like two wings on which
the human spirit rises to the contemplation of
truth. God has placed in the human heart a
desire to know the truth—to know Himself—
so that by knowing and loving God, men and
women may also come to the fullness of truth
about themselves.

6
Humanity's Future

Humanity's future depends on people who
rely on the truth and whose lives are en-
lightened by lofty moral principles that enable
their hearts to love to the point of sacrifice.

7
Every Life Is a Gift

Stand up for the life of the aged and the handicapped; stand up against attempts to promote
assisted suicide and euthanasia. Stand up for
marriage and family life. Stand up for purity.
Resist the pressures and temptations of a
world that too often tries to ignore a most
fundamental truth: that every life is a gift
from God our Creator and that we must give
an account to God of how we use it, either for
good or evil.

8
To Enter Many Hearts

Like Mary, we must allow the Holy Spirit to help us become intimate friends of Christ. Like Mary, we must put aside any fear in order to take Christ into the world in whatever we do—in marriage, as single people in the world, as students, as workers, as professional people. Through us, Christ wants to go to many places in the world and to enter many hearts.

9
Hidden

The Gospel must not be kept hidden because of fear or indifference. It was never meant to be hidden away in private. It has to be put on a stand so that people may see its light and give praise to our Heavenly Father.

10
Prophets of Life

I ask all the people of the world, who naturally and instinctively make love of life the horizon of their dreams and the rainbow of their hopes, to become prophets of life. Be such by your words and deeds, rebelling against the civilization of selfishness that often considers the human person a means rather than an end, sacrificing its dignity and feelings in the name of mere profit. Do so by concretely helping those who need us and who, without our help, would perhaps be tempted to resign themselves to despair.

11
Witnesses of Hope

We are witnesses. Witnesses of a shining faith;
of an active, patient, and kindly charity; of a
service for the many forms of poverty experi-
enced by contemporary humanity. Witnesses of
the hope that does not disappoint and of the
deep communion that reflects the life of God,
of the Trinity, of obedience, and of the Cross. In
short, witnesses of holiness, people of the
Beatitudes, called to be perfect as the Heavenly
Father is perfect.

12
Faith Is Demanding

How can we profess faith in God's Word, and
then refuse to let it inspire and direct our
thinking, our activity, our decisions, and our
responsibilities toward one another? Faith is
always demanding because faith leads us
beyond ourselves. Faith imparts a vision of
life's purpose and stimulates us to action.

13
What Does Christ Truly Ask of Us?

What does Christ truly ask of us? Jesus asks us to commit ourselves to proclaiming Him to our peers. Do not be afraid, because Jesus is with you! Do not be afraid of getting lost: The more we give of ourselves, the more we will find ourselves.

14
A Woman's Role in the Family

It is a disservice not only to children but also to
women and society itself when a woman is
made to feel guilty for wanting to remain in the
home and nurture and care for her children. It
is also necessary to counter the misconception
that the role of motherhood is oppressive to
women and that a commitment to her family,
particularly to her children, prevents a woman
from reaching personal fulfillment and from
having an influence in society. No response to
women's issues can ignore a woman's role in
the family or take lightly the fact that every
new life is entrusted to the protection and care
of the woman carrying it in her womb.

15
God Comes to Us

God comes to us in the things we know best
and can verify most easily, the things of our
everyday life.

16

The First School of Peace

Children very soon learn about life. They
watch and imitate the behavior of adults.
They rapidly learn love and respect for others,
but they also quickly absorb the poison of
violence and hatred. Family experiences
strongly condition the attitudes that children
will assume as adults. Consequently, if the
family is the place where children first
encounter the world, the family must be for
children the first school of peace.

17
The Gift of Peace

Become friends to those who have no friends.
Become family to those who have no family.
Become community to those who have no
community. If we want peace, we must reach
out to the poor. May the rich and poor of the
world recognize that we are all brothers and
sisters. May we all share what we have with one
another as children of the one God, who loves
everyone and who offers to everyone the gift
of peace.

18
Beyond Justice

More than 800 million people still suffer from malnutrition, and it is often difficult to find immediate solutions for improving these tragic situations. Nevertheless, we must seek them together so that we will no longer have, side by side, the starving and the wealthy, the very poor and the very rich, those who lack the necessary means and others who lavishly waste them. Such contrasts between poverty and wealth are intolerable for humanity.

19

All the Gold in the World

From the love of God, Christians learn to help
the poor and to share with them their own
material and spiritual goods. Such concern
not only provides those experiencing hardship
with material help but also represents an
opportunity for the spiritual growth of the
giver, who finds in it an incentive to become
detached from worldly goods. Remember,
every person is more valuable than all the gold
in the world.

20

Contribute Something

The crowds of starving people—children,
women, the elderly, immigrants, refugees, the
unemployed—raise to us their cry of suffering.
They implore us, hoping to be heard. How can
we not open our ears and our hearts and start
to make available those five loaves and two fish
that God has put into our hands? If each one of
us contributes something, we can all do something for the poor. Of course this will require
sacrifice, which calls for a deep inner conversion. Certainly it will involve changing our
exaggerated consumerist behavior, combating
hedonism, resisting attitudes of indifference
and the tendency to disregard our personal
responsibilities.

21
The Harmony of Creation

The contemplation of nature reveals not only the Creator but also our role in the world that He created. With faith it reveals the greatness of our dignity as creatures created in His image. In order to have life and have it abundantly, in order to reestablish the original harmony of creation, we must respect this divine image in all of creation, especially in human life itself.

22
A Genuine Contemplation

Many people are especially sensitive to the beauty of nature, and contemplating it inspires them spiritually. However, it must be a genuine contemplation. A contemplation that fails to reveal the face of a personal, intelligent, free, and loving God, but instead discerns merely the dim figure of an impersonal divinity or some cosmic force, does not suffice. We must not confuse the Creator with His creation.

23
A Moral Logic

We do not live in an irrational or meaningless world. On the contrary, there is a moral logic that is built into human life. We must find a way to discuss the human future intelligibly. The universal moral law written on the human heart is precisely that kind of "grammar" which is needed if the world is to engage in this discussion of its future. The politics of nations can never ignore the transcendent, spiritual dimension of the human experience.

24

The Longing for Freedom

The world has yet to learn how to live with
diversity. The fact of difference, and the reality
of "the other," can sometimes be felt as a bur-
den, or even as a threat. Amplified by historic
grievances and exacerbated by the manipula-
tions of the unscrupulous, the fear of difference
can lead to a denial of the very humanity of
"the other," with the result that people fall into
a cycle of violence in which no one is spared.
What will the world of the twenty-first century
be like? Shall we be able to make the most of
our past experiences and build peaceful coexis-
tence among the nations of the world? Will the
longing for freedom of so many people of the
earth be finally granted?

25
The Mystery of God

Every culture is an effort to ponder the mystery of the world and, in particular, of the human person: It is a way of giving expression to the transcendent dimension of human life. The heart of every culture is its approach to the greatest of all mysteries: the mystery of God.

26
Reading History

We must learn to read the history of other peoples without facile and partisan bias, making an effort to understand their point of view. If we set out on this journey, we shall come to see that mistakes are not all on one side. We shall see how history has sometimes been presented in a distorted and even manipulated way, with tragic results. History has been written almost exclusively as the narrative of men's achievements, when in fact its better part is most often molded by women's determined and persevering action for good. How much still needs to be said and written about man's enormous debt to woman in every other realm of social and cultural progress?

27
An Infinite Value

Recognition of someone as a human being can
never be based on the awareness or experience
we may have of him or her, but by the certitude
that they have an infinite value from concep-
tion, which comes to them from their
relationship with God. A human being has pri-
macy over all the ideas others have of them,
and their existence is absolute and not relative.

28

The Rule of Freedom

Freedom is not the absence of tyranny or oppression. Nor is freedom a license to do whatever we like. Freedom is ordered to the truth and is fulfilled in humanity's quest for truth and in humanity's living the truth. Truth—beginning with the truth of our redemption through the cross and resurrection of Jesus Christ—is the root and rule of freedom, the foundation and measure of all liberation. Ultimately, freedom can be a risk. If freedom does not obey the truth, it can crush us.

29
The Cornerstone

The mystery of the Incarnation has given a tremendous impetus to humanity's thought and artistic genius. Precisely by reflecting on the union of the two natures, human and divine, in the Person of the Incarnate Word, Christian thinkers have come to explain the concept of a person as the unique and unrepeatable center of freedom and responsibility, whose inalienable dignity must be realized. This concept of the person has proved to be the cornerstone for any genuinely human civilization.

30

The Last Times

Everything that will happen until the end of the
world will be no more than an extension and
unfolding of what happened on the day when the
battered body of the crucified Lord was raised
by the power of the Spirit and became in turn
the wellspring of the Spirit for all humanity.
Christians know that there is no need to wait for
another time of salvation since, however long
the world may last, they are already living in the
last times. Not only we the Church but also the
very cosmos itself and all of history are cease-
lessly ruled and governed by the glorified
Christ. It is this life force which propels creation, "groaning in labor pains until now," toward
the goal of its full redemption.

31
The Living Presence

"I am with you always, to the end of the age." This promise of Christ is the sustaining secret of our life and the wellspring of our hope. As the day of Resurrection, Sunday is not only the remembrance of a past event: It is a celebration of the living presence of the risen Lord in the midst of His own people.

32
The Firstfruits of the Church

At Sunday Mass, Christians relive with particular intensity the experience of the apostles on the evening of Easter when the risen Lord appeared to them as they were gathered together. In a sense, the people of God of all times were present in that small nucleus of disciples, the firstfruits of the Church. Through their testimony, every generation of believers hears the greeting of Christ, rich with the messianic gift of peace, won by His blood and offered with His Spirit: "Peace be with you."

33
Lasting Peace

Lasting peace is marked by mutual acceptance and a capacity to forgive from the heart. We all need to be forgiven by others, so we all must be ready to forgive. Asking for and granting forgiveness is something profoundly worthy of humanity; sometimes it is the only way out of situations marked by age-old and violent hatred.

34
A Radical Conversion

Can we be fully reconciled with Christ without being fully reconciled among ourselves? Can we bear joint and effective witness to Christ if we are not reconciled with one another? Can we be reconciled with one another without forgiving one another? Forgiveness is the condition for reconciliation. But this cannot take place without interior transformation and conversion, which is the work of grace. We need to be able to confront ourselves, to undertake a rigorous examination of conscience—this is the indispensable premise for a radical conversion that can transform our lives.

35
Justice

An essential prerequisite for forgiveness and reconciliation is justice, which finds its ultimate foundation in the law of God and in His plan of love and mercy for humanity. Understood in this way, justice is not limited to establishing what is right between the parties in conflict but looks above all to reestablishing authentic relationships with God, with oneself, and with others. Thus there is no contradiction between forgiveness and justice. Forgiveness neither eliminates nor lessens the need for the reparation which justice requires, but seeks to reintegrate individuals and groups into society, and states into the community of nations. No punishment can suppress the inalienable dignity of those who have committed evil. The door to repentance and rehabilitation must always remain open.

36
The Measure with Which
We Shall All Be Judged

Throughout His life Jesus proclaimed God's forgiveness, but He also taught the need for mutual forgiveness as the condition for obtaining it. In the Lord's Prayer, He makes us pray: "Forgive us our trespasses as we forgive those who trespass against us." With that "as," He places in our hands the measure with which we shall all be judged by God.

37

An Act of Love

God alone is absolute truth. But He made the
human heart open to the desire for truth,
which He then fully revealed in His Incarnate
Son. Hence we are all called to live the truth.
Where lies and falsehood are sown, suspicion
and division flourish. Forgiveness, far from pre-
cluding the search for truth, actually requires
it. The evil that has been done must be
acknowledged and as far as possible corrected.
Forgiveness, in its truest and highest form, is a
free act of love. But precisely because it is an
act of love, it has its own intrinsic demands: the
first of which is respect for the truth.

38
A Healing of Memories

The truth is that we cannot remain prisoners of the past; people need a sort of "healing of memories" so that past evils will not come back again. This does not mean forgetting past events; it means reexamining them with a new attitude and learning precisely from the experience of suffering that only love can build upwards, whereas hatred produces only devastation and ruin.

39

The Freedom We Yearn For

In a culture that holds that no universally valid truths are possible, nothing is absolute. Therefore, in the end, objective goodness and evil no longer really matter. Good comes to mean what is pleasing or useful at a particular moment. Evil means what contradicts our subjective wishes. Each person can build a private system of values. Only by listening to the voice of God in our most intimate being, and by acting in accordance with its directions, will we reach the freedom we yearn for. As Jesus said, only the truth will make us free. And the truth is not the fruit of each individual's imagination. God gave us intelligence to know the truth and the will to achieve what is morally good.

40
The Bond

Prayer is the bond that most effectively unites us. It is through prayer that believers meet one another at a level where inequalities, misunderstandings, bitterness, and hostility are overcome, namely before God, the Lord and Father of us all.

41
Absolute Trust

To learn who the Father is means learning what absolute trust is. "To learn the Father" means acquiring the certainty that He does not refuse us even when everything—materially and psychologically—seems to indicate refusal. He never refuses us.

42

Learning the Father

"Our Father, who art in heaven . . ." According to these words everything is reduced to a single concept: to learn to pray means "to learn the Father." If we learn the Father in the full sense of the word, we have learned everything.

43
The Center

Prayer is not one occupation among many, but is at the center of our life in Christ. It turns our attention away from ourselves and directs it to the Lord. Prayer fills the mind with truth and gives hope to the heart.

44

The Breath of the Divine Life

The breath of the divine life, the Holy Spirit, in its simplest and most common manner, expresses itself and makes itself felt in prayer. Wherever people are praying in the world, there the Holy Spirit is, the living breath of prayer. Prayer is also the voice of all those who have no voice. Prayer is the revelation of the abyss that is at the heart of humanity: a depth that comes from God and which only God can fill.

45

Life Is a Talent

Life is a talent entrusted to us so that we can transform it and increase it, making it a gift to others. No person is an iceberg drifting on the ocean of history. Each one of us belongs to a great family, in which we each have our own place and our own role to play.

46

The Reflection of the Creator

Have faith in the God of life, who has created every individual as a wonder. It is the outlook of those who see life in its deeper meaning, who grasp its utter gratuitousness, its beauty, and its invitation to freedom and responsibility. It is the outlook of those who do not presume to take possession of reality but instead accept it as a gift, discovering in all things the reflection of the Creator and seeing in every person his living image.

47

Bodies and Souls

In our bodies we are mere specks in the vast
created universe, but by virtue of our souls
we transcend the whole material world.

48

The Mosaic of Charity

Selfishness makes us deaf and dumb; love opens
our eyes and hearts, enabling us to make an
original and irreplaceable contribution that—
together with the thousands of deeds of so
many brothers and sisters, often distant and
unknown—converges to form the mosaic of
charity that can change the tide of history.

49

The Mystery of Grace

It is not simply a case of humanity seeking
God, but of God who comes in Person to speak
to each of us of Himself and to show us the
path by which He may be reached. The
Incarnate Word is the fulfillment of the yearning present in all the religions of mankind: this
fulfillment is brought about by God Himself
and transcends all our human expectations. It is
the mystery of grace.

50
In Search of Us

God goes in search of us. Jesus speaks of this search as the finding of a lost sheep. It is a search that begins in the heart of God and culminates in the Incarnation of the Word. God goes in search of us because He loves us eternally in the Word and wishes to raise us in Christ to the dignity of adoptive sons and daughters. We are His special possessions in a way unlike any other creature by virtue of a choice made in love: God seeks us out, moved by His fatherly heart.

51

The Meaning of the Redemption

Why does God seek us out? Because we have
turned away from Him, hiding ourselves as
Adam and Eve did among the trees of the
Garden of Eden. We have allowed ourselves to
be led astray by the enemy of God. Satan
deceived us, persuading us that he, too, was a
god, that he, like God, was capable of knowing
good and evil, ruling the world according to his
own will without having to take into account
the divine will. Going in search of us through
His Son, God wishes to persuade us to abandon
the paths of evil that lead us farther and farther
afield. Making us abandon those paths means
making us understand that we are taking the
wrong path; it means overcoming the evil
that is everywhere found in human history.
Overcoming evil: this is the meaning of the
Redemption.

52
Authentic Freedom

Jesus Christ meets the men and women of every age, including our own, with the same words: "You will know the truth, and the truth will make you free." These words contain both a fundamental requirement and a warning: the requirement of an honest relationship with regard to truth as a condition for authentic freedom, and the warning to avoid every kind of illusory freedom, that is, every freedom that fails to enter into the whole truth about our lives and our world.

53
The Life of God

Jesus came to provide the ultimate answer to
the yearning for life and the infinite that God
poured into our hearts at creation. Jesus pro-
claims, "I am . . . the life" and "I came that they
may have life." But what life? Jesus' intention
was clear: the very life of God, which surpasses
all the possible aspirations of the human heart.
The fact is that through the grace of our
Baptism we are all God's children.

54
True Life

Our daily experience tells us that life is marked
by sin and threatened by death, despite the
desire for good which beats in all our hearts
and the desire for life which courses through
our veins. We discover that everything within
us impels us to overcome the temptations of
superficiality and despair. It is then that we are
called to become disciples of the One who infi-
nitely transcends all.

55

The Church's Function

The Church's fundamental function in every age, and particularly in ours, is to direct our gaze toward the mystery of God, to help all men and women to be familiar with the profundity of the Redemption taking place in Christ Jesus. In Christ and through Christ, God has revealed Himself fully to humanity and has definitively drawn close to it; at the same time, in Christ and through Christ we have acquired full awareness of the surpassing worth of our own humanity, and of the meaning of our existence. All of us who are Christ's followers must therefore meet and unite around Him.

56
Christ the Teacher

Christ's words, His parables, and His arguments are never separable from His life and His very being. The whole of Christ's life was a continual teaching. His silences, His miracles, His gestures, His prayer, His love for people, His special affection for the little and the poor, His acceptance of the total sacrifice on the Cross for the redemption of the world, and His resurrection are the actualization of His word and the fulfillment of revelation. Hence, for Christians the crucifix is one of the most sublime and popular images of Christ the Teacher.

57

The Teacher Who Will Come Again in Glory

Christ is the Teacher who reveals God to humanity and humanity to itself. He is the Teacher who saves, sanctifies, and guides, who lives, who speaks, rouses, moves, redresses, judges, forgives, and goes with us day by day on the path of history, the Teacher who will come again in glory.

58
The Gospel of Life

To each one of us Christ says: "I send you." Why is He sending us? Because men and women the world over long for true liberation and fulfillment. The poor seek justice and solidarity; the oppressed demand freedom and dignity; the blind cry out for light and truth. We are not being sent out to proclaim some abstract truth. The Gospel is not a theory or an ideology. The Gospel is life!

59

Who You Really Are

There is a message that we have to proclaim to
the modern world, especially to the least fortu-
nate, to the homeless and dispossessed, to the
sick, the outcasts, to those who suffer at the
hands of others. To each one we must say: Look
to Jesus Christ in order to see who you really
are in the eyes of God.

60
The True Face of Jesus Christ

Jesus says to us: "I am sending you to your families, to your parishes, to your movements and associations, to your countries, to ancient cultures and modern civilization, so that you will proclaim the dignity of every human being, as revealed by me, the Son of Man." If you defend the inalienable dignity of every human being, you will be revealing to the world the true face of Jesus Christ, who is one with every man, every woman, and every child, no matter how poor, no matter how weak or handicapped.

61

How Does Jesus Send Us?

How does Jesus send us? He promises neither
sword nor money nor power. He gives us
instead peace and truth. He sends us out with
the powerful message of His Paschal Mystery,
with the truth of His cross and resurrection.
That is all He gives us, and that is all we need.

62
Seek Jesus

Seek Jesus. Let your life be a continual, sincere search for Him, without ever tiring, without ever abandoning the undertaking, even though darkness should fall on your spirit, temptations beset you, and grief and incomprehension wring your heart. These are the things that are part of life here below; they are inevitable, but they can also be beneficial because they mature our spirit. We must never turn back, even if it should seem to you that the light of Christ is fading. On the contrary, continue seeking with renewed faith and greater generosity.

63

A Mark of His Passing

We must deepen our knowledge of Jesus,
listening to the word of the Lord and reading
the pages of the Gospels. Try to discover where
He is, and you will be able to gather from
everyone some detail that will indicate it to
you, that will tell you where He lives. Ask souls
that are meek, repentant, generous, humble,
and hidden; ask your brothers and sisters, far
and near, because you will find in everyone
something that indicates Jesus to you. Ask,
above all, your soul and your conscience,
because they will be able to indicate to you, in
an unmistakable way, a mark of His passing, a
trace of His power and His love.

64
Let Your Soul Be Ready

Let your soul be ready to see those parts of His goodness that God has sown in creatures. To seek Him every day means possessing Him a little more every day, being admitted a little at a time to intimacy with Him; and then you will be able to understand better the sound of His voice, the meaning of His language, the reason for His coming to earth and for His sacrifice on the Cross.

65

A God Who Reveals Himself

In Christ, religion is no longer a blind search
for God but the response of faith to a God
who reveals Himself. We speak to God as our
Creator and Father, a response made possible
by Christ Jesus—the one Man in whom God
speaks to each individual person and by whom
each individual person is enabled to respond
to God.

66
The New Beginning

Jesus Christ is the new beginning of everything.
In Him all things come into their own; they are
taken up and given back to the Creator from
whom they first came. Christ is thus the
fulfillment of the yearning of all the world's
religions, and, as such, He is their sole and
definitive completion. In Christ, God speaks to
humanity of Himself, in Christ all of humanity
and the whole of creation speaks of itself to
God—indeed, it gives itself to God.

67
Be Humble

Be humble before the Almighty. Maintain the
sense of mystery, because there always remains
the infinite between God and us. Remember
that before God and His revelation it is not so
much a question of understanding with our
own limited reason, but rather of loving.

68
May Our Faith Be Strong

May our faith be strong; may it not hesitate,
not waver, before the doubts, the uncertainties
that philosophical systems or fashionable movements would like to suggest to us. May our
faith be certain. May it be founded on the Word
of God; on deep knowledge of the Gospel message, and especially of the life, person, and
work of Christ; and also on the interior witness
of the Holy Spirit.

69
Active Faith

Let our faith be active, let it manifest itself and take on concrete shape in laborious and generous charity toward our brothers and sisters who live crushed in sorrow and in need; let it be manifested in our serene adherence to the teaching of the truth; let it be expressed in our availability for all those tasks that we are called upon to participate in the building up of the Kingdom of God.

70

Faith Is a Decision

Christian faith is not simply a set of proposi-
tions to be accepted with intellectual assent.
Faith is a lived knowledge of Christ, a living
remembrance of His commandments, and a
truth to be lived out. A word is not truly
received until it is put into practice. Faith is a
decision involving one's whole existence. It is
an encounter, a dialogue, a communion of love
and of life between the believer and Jesus
Christ, the Way, the Truth, and the Life. It
entails an act of trusting abandonment to
Christ, which enables us to live as He lived,
in profound love of God and of our brothers
and sisters.

71
Fiat in Faith

The mystery of the Incarnation was accomplished when Mary uttered her fiat "Let it be with me according to your word," which made possible the granting of her Son's desire. Mary uttered this fiat in faith. In faith she entrusted herself to God without reserve and "devoted herself totally as the handmaid of the Lord to the person and work of her Son." And—as the Fathers of the Church teach—she conceived this Son in her mind before she conceived Him in her womb: precisely in faith. Rightly therefore does Elizabeth praise Mary: "And blessed is she who believed that there would be a fulfillment of what was spoken to her by the Lord."

72
Abandon Oneself

To believe means to abandon oneself to the truth of the Word of the living God, knowing and humbly recognizing "how unsearchable are his judgments and how inscrutable his ways." Mary stands at the very center of those "inscrutable . . . ways" and "unsearchable . . . judgments" of God, conforms herself to them in the dim light of faith, accepting fully and with a ready heart everything that is decreed in the divine plan.

73

Invisible Grace

Baptism is a sacrament, a visible sign of invisible grace; it is the door through which God acts in the human soul to unite it to Himself in Christ and the Church. He makes it share in Redemption. He infuses new life into it. He makes it part of the communion of saints. He opens the way to the other sacraments. Baptism is a rebirth by which a child of man becomes a child of God.

74

Joined Together

Regenerated as children in the Son of God, the baptized are inseparably joined together as "members of Christ and members of the body of the Church." Baptism symbolizes and brings about a mystical but real incorporation into the crucified and glorious Body of Christ. Through the sacrament Jesus unites the baptized to His death so as to unite the recipient to His resurrection. The "old man" is stripped away for reclothing with the "new man," that is, with Jesus Himself: For "as many of you as were baptized into Christ have clothed yourselves with Christ." The result is that "we, who are many, are one body in Christ."

75

Catechesis

The Church has always considered catechesis one of her primary tasks. Before Christ ascended to His Father after His resurrection, He gave His apostles a final command—to make disciples of all nations and to teach them to observe all that He had commanded. He thus entrusted them with the mission and power to proclaim to humanity what they had heard, what they had seen with their eyes, what they had looked upon and touched with their hands concerning the Word of Life. He also entrusted them with the mission and power to explain with authority what He had taught them, His words and actions, His signs and commandments. And He gave them the Spirit to fulfill this mission.

76

The Heart of Catechesis

The heart of catechesis is, in essence, a Person, the Person of Jesus of Nazareth, "the only Son from the Father . . . full of grace and truth," who suffered and died for us, and who now, after rising, is living with us forever. It is Jesus who is "the way, and the truth, and the life," and Christian living consists in following Christ. Catechizing is a way to lead a person to study the mystery of Christ in all its dimensions.

77

Life of the Faithful

The specific goal of catechesis is to develop an
as-yet initial faith and to nourish, day by day,
the Christian life of the faithful. It is a matter of
giving growth, at the level of knowledge and in
life, to the seed of faith sown by the Holy
Spirit. Catechesis aims at developing understanding of the mystery of Christ in the light of
God's Word, so that the whole of a person's
humanity is infused by that Word.

78

Laborers in His Vineyard

God calls us and sends us forth as laborers in His vineyard. He calls us and sends us forth to work for the coming of His Kingdom in history. In fact, from eternity God has thought of each of us and has loved us as unique individuals. Every one of us He has called by name. However, only in the unfolding of the personal history of our lives and its events is the eternal plan of God revealed to each of us. It is a gradual process; one that happens day by day.

79

The Will of the Lord

To be able to discover the actual will of the
Lord in our lives always involves the following: receptive listening to the Word of God
and the Church, fervent and constant prayer,
recourse to a wise and loving spiritual guide,
and faithful discernment of the gifts and tal-
ents given us by God.

80
Discerning God's Call

In the life of each member of the faithful there are particularly significant and decisive moments for discerning God's call and embracing the mission entrusted by Him. No one must forget that the Lord, as the Master of the laborers in the vineyard, calls at every hour of life so as to make His holy will more precisely and explicitly known. Therefore, the fundamental and continuous attitude of the disciple should be one of vigilance and a conscious attentiveness to the voice of God.

81

Doing What God Wants

It is not a question of simply *knowing* what God wants from each of us in the various situations of life. The individual must *do* what God wants.

82
Every Area of Our Lives

There cannot be two parallel lives in the existence of the faithful: on the one hand, our so-called spiritual life, with its values and demands; and on the other, our so-called secular life, that is, life in a family, at work, in social relationships, in the responsibilities of public life, and in culture. Every area of our lives, as different as they are, enters into the plan of God, who desires that these very areas be the places where the love of Christ is revealed and realized for both the glory of the Father and service of others.

83
Embracing the Beatitudes

Life lived according to the Spirit stirs up every baptized person and requires each to follow and imitate Jesus Christ. We do this by embracing the Beatitudes; in listening and meditating on the Word of God; in conscious and active participation in the liturgical and sacramental life of the Church; in personal prayer; in family or in community; in the hunger and thirst for justice; in the practice of the commandment of love in all circumstances of life; and in service to the brethren, especially the least, the poor, and the suffering.

84

Turning to the Bible

In order to recognize who Christ truly is, we should turn with renewed interest to the Bible. In the revealed text it is the Heavenly Father Himself who comes to us in love and who dwells with us, disclosing to us the nature of His only-begotten Son and His plan of salvation for humanity.

85
One of Our Deepest Needs

"Lord, teach us to pray." When, on the slopes
of the Mount of Olives, the apostles addressed
Jesus with these words, they were not asking an
ordinary question, but with spontaneous trust,
they were expressing one of the deepest needs
of the human heart.

86

Trusting Abandonment

As Christians, we know that for us prayer is as essential as breathing, and once we have tasted the sweetness of intimate conversation with God, we do not hesitate to immerse ourselves in it with trusting abandonment.

87
Prayer and Action

The deep unity between prayer and action is at the basis of all spiritual renewal, especially among the faithful. It is at the basis of the great enterprises of evangelization and construction of the world according to God's plan.

88
In, but Not Of

All of us are trying to live a really Christian and evangelical life as Christians "in the world" without being "of the world." This apostolic life calls for effective openness to our various environments in order to cause the evangelical "leaven" to penetrate them. It involves multiple activities and responsibilities to be assumed in all areas of human life: the family, professions, society, culture, and politics. It is by assuming these responsibilities competently and in deep union with God that we will fulfill our vocation as Christians: that we will sanctify ourselves and sanctify the world.

89
Finding Meaning

A contemplative outlook does not give in to
discouragement when confronted by those who
are sick, suffering, outcast, or at death's door.
Instead, in all these situations it feels chal-
lenged to find meaning, and precisely in the
face of every person it finds a call to encounter,
to dialogue, and for solidarity.

90
Necessary Detachment

Food and drink are indispensable for us to live. We must use them, but we may not abuse them. The tradition of abstention from food and drink has as its purpose to introduce into our existence not only the necessary balance but also detachment from what might be defined as a "consumer attitude." In our times this attitude has become one of the characteristics of civilization and, in particular, of Western civilization.

91
Fasting

Fasting is more than mere abstinence from nourishment or material food. Fasting is a symbol, a sign, a serious and stimulating call to accept or to make renunciations. What renunciations? Renunciation of the "ego," that is, of so many caprices or unhealthy aspirations; renunciation of one's own defects, of impetuous passion and desires. Fasting is being able to say no, bluntly and firmly, to what is suggested or asked by pride, selfishness, and vice; listening to one's own conscience; respecting the good of others; remaining faithful to God's holy law.

92

Subject to Temptation

The Lord Jesus allowed Himself to be tempted by the evil one in order to show us how we should behave when subjected to temptation. For those who beseech the Father not to be tempted beyond their own strength, being subjected to temptation does not mean that they have sinned. Rather it is an opportunity for growing in fidelity and consistency through humility and watchfulness.

93
Carrying the Cross

Sweat and toil, which work necessarily involves in the present condition of the human race, presents everyone with the possibility of sharing lovingly in the work that Christ came to do. This work of salvation came about through suffering and death on a Cross. By enduring the toil of work in union with Christ crucified for us, we collaborate with the Son of God for the redemption of humanity. We show ourselves to be true disciples of Christ by carrying the Cross every day in the activities we are called upon to perform. The Christian finds in human work a small part of the Cross of Christ and accepts it in the same spirit of redemption in which Christ accepted His Cross for us.

Opening Our Hearts

Even if we do not have at our disposal riches and concrete capacities to meet the needs of our neighbors, we cannot feel dispensed from opening our hearts to their necessities and relieving them as far as possible. Remember the widow's mite. She threw into the treasury of the temple only two small coins, but with them, all her great love, for "she out of her poverty has put in everything she had, all she had to live on." It is, above all, the interior value of the gift that counts: the readiness to share everything, the readiness to give oneself. St. Paul writes: "If I give away all my possessions . . . but do not have love, I gain nothing."

95
The Reality of Suffering

The reality of suffering is ever before our eyes and often in the body, soul, and heart of each of us. Pain has always been a great riddle of human existence. However, ever since Jesus redeemed the world by His passion and death, a new perspective has been opened: through suffering one can grow in self-giving and attain the highest degree of love because of Him who "loved us and gave himself up for us."

96
Earthly Suffering

Jesus did not hesitate to proclaim the blessedness of those who suffer: "Blessed are those who mourn, for they will be comforted. . . . Blessed are those who are persecuted for righteousness' sake, for theirs is the kingdom of heaven. Blessed are you when people revile you and persecute you and utter all kinds of evil against you falsely on my account. Rejoice and be glad, for your reward is great in heaven." This blessedness can only be understood if we admit that human life is not limited to the time spent on earth, but is wholly directed to perfect joy and fullness of life in the hereafter. Earthly suffering, when accepted in love, is like a bitter kernel containing the seed of new life, the treasure of divine glory to be given us in eternity.

97
Suffering as Offering

A basic principle of our Christian faith is the fruitfulness of suffering and, hence, the call of all those who suffer to unite themselves with Christ's redemptive sacrifice. Suffering thus becomes an offering, an oblation; this has happened and still does in so many holy souls. Especially those who are oppressed by apparently senseless moral suffering find in Jesus' moral suffering the meaning of their own trials, and they go with Him into Gethsemane. In Him they find the strength to accept pain with holy abandon and trusting obedience to the Father's will. And they feel, rising from within their hearts, the prayer of Gethsemane: "But let it be as you would have it, Father, not as I."

98

To God for Guidance

O God, You are our Creator. You are good and Your mercy knows no bounds. To You arises the praise of every creature. You have given us an inner law by which we must live. To do Your will is our task. To follow Your ways is to know peace of heart. Guide us on all the paths we travel upon this earth. Free us from all the evil tendencies that lead our hearts away from Your will. Never allow us to stray from You; help us to be included among Your chosen ones on the last day.

99
To the Spirit

May the Holy Spirit, the Spirit of Pentecost,
help us to clarify what is ambiguous, to give
warmth to what is indifferent, to enlighten in
us what is obscure, and to be before the world
true and generous witnesses of Christ's love,
for no one can live without love.

100

That They May All Be One

Let us raise our prayer and say together: "That they may all be one." That Christians may bear common witness to the service of His Kingdom. That all Christian communities may unite in the pursuit of full unity. That the perfect unity of all Christians may be realized so that God may be glorified by all people in Christ the Lord. That all peoples on earth may overcome conflicts and selfishness and find full reconciliation and peace in the Kingdom of God. Remember Your Church, O Lord; preserve her from all evil; make her perfect in Your love; sanctify her and gather her from the four winds into Your Kingdom, which You have prepared for her. For Yours is the power and the glory forever and ever.